My Secret World

Fantastic Fairies

Kay Woodward

Illustrated by Strawberrie Donnelly

PUFFIN

PUFFIN BOOKS

Published by the Penguin Group
Penguin Books Ltd, 80 Strand, London WC2R 0RL, England
Penguin Group (USA) Inc., 375 Hudson Street, New York, New York 10014, USA
Penguin Group (Canada), 90 Eglinton Avenue East, Suite 700,
Toronto, Ontario, Canada M4P 2Y3
Penguin Ireland, 25 St Stephen's Green, Dublin 2, Ireland
(a division of Penguin Books Ltd)
Penguin Group (Australia), 250 Camberwell Road, Camberwell, Victoria 3124,
Australia (a division of Pearson Australia Group Pty Ltd)
Penguin Books India Pvt Ltd, 11 Community Centre, Panchsheel Park,
New Delhi – 110 017, India
Penguin Group (NZ), cnr Airborne and Rosedale Roads, Albany, Auckland 1310,
New Zealand (a division of Pearson New Zealand Ltd)
Penguin Books (South Africa) (Pty) Ltd, 24 Sturdee Avenue, Rosebank,
Johannesburg 2196, South Africa

Penguin Books Ltd, Registered Offices: 80 Strand, London WC2R 0RL, England

www.penguin.com

First published 2005
1

Text copyright © Kay Woodward, 2005
Illustrations copyright © Strawberrie Donnelly, 2005
All rights reserved

The moral right of the author and illustrator has been asserted

Set in Weiss

Made and printed in England by Clays Ltd, St Ives plc

British Library Cataloguing in Publication Data
A CIP catalogue record for this book is available from the British Library

ISBN 0–141–31995–X

Contents

Welcome to the secret world of fairies . . .

Do you believe in fairies? Have you ever wanted to meet a real fairy or wished that you had your very own magic fairy wand? Do you dream of taking off to Fairyland with a wiggle of your fairy wings?

Fairies are totally fantastic creatures. They are unlike anything else in this world – or any other world. They are lighter than air, faster than lightning and more powerful than a space rocket. And they're filled to the brim with pure magic.

But what are they really like? Where do they live?
What's the best way to find a fairy? To discover the
answers, all you have to do is follow these three
magic steps:

1. Find a comfy chair.
2. Put your feet up.
3. Read on . . .

Chapter One
All about fairies

She is smaller than a butterfly. Her wings are made of the most delicate gossamer – so fine that the sunlight gleams through as if they were not there. Yet she flies faster than the swooping swallow, twirling and whirling through the air. Suddenly, the tiny creature lands on a flower bud and lightly taps her wand. The bud unfolds into the most beautiful flower. In a twinkling, the fairy vanishes.

Fairies are mysterious magical beings that live all around. And, without the wave of a fairy's wand or a sprinkling of fairy dust, the world would be a duller, less sparkly place.

⭐ Earth, air, water and fire

There are many varieties of fairy, but they can be grouped together into four main types:

Earth fairies prefer to keep their feet firmly on the ground – or under it. They don't have wings. Most of them aren't pretty at all. But they can dish out buckets and buckets of magic – if they're in the right mood.

Air fairies are delicate, delightful and they like to charm. They love to dress in pink. These winged fairies are the only ones who can fly.

Water fairies live in babbling brooks and wide oceans. They also like to relax behind waterfalls – this is a really good place to spot them.

Fire fairies are at home in hot, fiery places like volcanoes, where they relax by swimming in scalding lava. Ouch!

Fairy magic

No matter where they live, all fairies really can do magic. It's what they like doing best. And they're pretty good at it too. A single fairy has enough magic to light the fairy lights on about 500 Christmas trees — and that's before breakfast.

Fairy magic is not something that can be easily taught. A magic wand and a handful of fairy dust will help a fairy to perform enchantments, but the first burst of magic has to come from deep inside. They have to *feel* the magic.

Magical fairy secrets

✿ The summer solstice is the longest day of the year — and the most mystical. Make a note in your diary to do some truly magical things on 21 June. You'll be glad you did.

✿ The Sugar Plum Fairy is a real celebrity fairy. She appears in a famous ballet called **The Nutcracker** and even dances to her very own tune.

✿ Did you know that Jack Frost is a fairy? He visits during the night and sprinkles icy-cold fairy dust over everything in sight.

Chapter Two
Here, there and everywhere!

On the rock sits the most amazing of all fairy folk – the mermaid. Her long hair hangs like a silken curtain around her beautiful face. Waves splash gently against her silvery tail.
Then she begins to sing a haunting, sad tune that tells of the sea, the wind and the stars.
In the distance, a boat appears – its sailors cannot resist the mermaid's song.

Fairies are everywhere – it's official. Some are small and cute, while others are big and scary. In Germany, you'll find elegant water sprites called nixes. In Scotland, there are brownies, who help around the house. In Ireland, wood sprites dance among the trees.

☆ Fairy dictionary

Hundreds of different kinds of fairies flit, float and twinkle around the world. But do you know the difference between an elf and a pixie? Here are some of the fairies you're most likely to come across ...

Dwarfs

These fairies live inside the mountains and mines of Scandinavia. No taller than 50 cm, they usually look like grumpy old men with long, straggly beards.

Elves

These German fairies look just like mini humans. A few elves are kind and helpful, but most are very naughty indeed. The most wicked elves are said to whisk away human children and leave fairy children in their place ...

Flying Fairies

They are dainty, glitzy and very twinkly and usually no bigger than your thumb.

Gnomes

Gnomes have pointy hats and pointy beards. They live deep underground, where they guard top-secret treasure.

Goblins

They're mean, they're
mischievous and
they pull covers off
sleeping humans.
So, if your duvet
is on the floor when
you wake, the goblins might
have paid you a visit during the night ...

Imps

When gloves and
keys go missing,
imps are usually to
blame. Although
they're naughty, they're
never nasty. The best way to
stop imps from pinching your socks is to play
music to them – these fairy minxes are very
fond of all music, including the latest hits!

Leprechauns

The most famous of all the Irish fairies look like little old men and they just love the colour green. Leprechauns also find time to make special shoes called brogues.

Mermaids

The most beautiful of all sea creatures, mermaids are said to lure sailors with enchanting music. From the waist up, a mermaid looks just like a woman, but instead of legs she has a glittery, swishy tail.

Pixies

Like leprechauns, pixies love to wear green. In their spare time, they like to blow out candles. Watch out for them on your birthday – you don't want them to get to your birthday cake before you do.

Magical fairy secrets

❀ The word leprechaun comes from an old Irish word – luchopán – which means 'little body'.

❀ Sprite is another word for a fairy. It comes from the word 'spiritus', which means spirit.

❀ Oak, ash and hawthorns are fairy trees. You must never cut one down – to do so would disturb the fairies and bring bad luck.

Chapter Three
Fairyland

The buttercups have filled with raindrops during the April shower. The fairy tips up a flower and takes a long, wet gulp. Then she hears the thud of feet. A human — at dawn? But it is. A girl with dark curls and dark eyes. And she is looking the fairy's way. The fairy acts quickly, whirling an invisibility enchantment all around herself. The girl frowns, shakes her head and moves on — and the trembling fairy heaves a sigh of relief. She's safe.

An incredible number of fairies whizz around the world – about 12 million according to the last fairy census. So we should be able to spot them everywhere, right? Wrong. When fairies visit the human world, they do their very best to stay out of sight.

Where fairies live

Fairyland is very close to the human world. In fact, the two worlds are so close they actually touch at extra-magical spots such as waterfalls and old stone bridges. Here, it is quite easy for a fairy to skip from one world to the other. Unfortunately, it's very difficult for a human to perform the same feat.

Fairyland itself is a totally enchanted place where colours are softer and sounds are quieter. A pale sun shines in daytime, while at night there's always a full moon. Ribbons of mist wrap themselves around the many trees, which

stretch as far as the eye can see. And everywhere, there are fairies.

⭐ The fairy isle

Ireland is a truly magical place – perhaps the
most magical in the world. It is home to all sorts
of fairy folk, who are known as *sídhe*. (If you
want to sound like a real fairy expert, remember
to pronounce it *shee*.) A pooka is an Irish fairy

who's a little like a goblin. A banshee is a noisy fairy – her wails foretell bad luck. And if you're ever lucky enough to find a leprechaun, make sure that you don't look away. If you meet the leprechaun's gaze for long enough, he must take you to his crock of gold. (This is usually hidden at the very end of a rainbow.)

There's fairy evidence all over Ireland – you just have to know where to look. Brughs are dotted around the countryside. They may look like mounds of earth, but fairies once dwelled deep inside them. Fairy mountains – including

Knockfierna in County Limerick – were once home to fairy kings and queens.

Magical fairy secrets

❀ Fairyland can be a dangerous place. People should take care never to eat a single crumb or drink a single drop when they visit. If they do, they may never return to the world of humans. Ever.

❀ According to legend, the magical island off the west coast of Ireland – called Tír na nÓg – is home to Irish fairy folk. Those who live there will always be young.

❀ Groups of ancient stones – like those at Stonehenge – are surrounded by pure magic. If you visit, remember to check around the bottom of these stones – fairies have been known to shelter there.

Chapter Four
Bad fairies!

*G*reer sighed. Everything that could have gone wrong this morning had gone wrong. Her alarm clock hadn't gone off. She'd lost the tie from her school uniform. And the last page of her homework was missing. It was almost as if mischievous elves had crept into her room during the night and fiddled with everything. But that couldn't be true...could it?

Have you ever wondered how fluff-covered sweets find their way to the bottom of your pockets? Or why fizzy drinks spill when you haven't touched them? How about tiny treasures that mysteriously go missing in your bedroom?

Every single one of these odd happenings might be the work of fairies!

⭐ Bad behaviour

Not all fairies spend their time flying merrily from problem to problem, putting everything right with a wave of their wand. Some fairies are bad. Really bad ...

Trolls — some of the nastiest fairies around — are very talented at becoming invisible. But this does not make them bad — it's what they do *when* they're invisible that makes them bad. They are nasty, rotten thieves. Trolls like nothing better than vanishing from sight, then stealing gold and crystal to decorate their own homes.

But if a troll ever steals your belongings, there's a very simple way to get rid of him (or her). Trolls hate noise.

All you have to do is arm yourself with a saucepan and a big wooden spoon and BANG, BANG, BANG it as loud as you can, for as long as you can. When you stop banging, the troll will have vanished for good.

⭐ *When good fairies turn bad...*

It's hard work being sweet and kind, doing good and – of course – sprinkling fairy dust wherever you go. (A bag of fairy dust can weigh as much as a bag of sugar, which is very heavy indeed if you're only 5 cm tall.) So, it's not surprising that even the very nicest, most helpful fairies have their off days.

For example, elves can be either helpful or mischievous. German fairies called kobolds help around the house, but they

can't resist pushing people over when they bend to tie their shoelaces! Goblins often keep people awake by banging pots and pans at night, but they also leave presents for children who have been good.

The bad guys

The boggart and the bogle are two of the nastiest, noisiest fairies of all. They wait until night … when everyone is asleep … and then … when it is really quiet … they begin TO MAKE NOISE! (To get some idea of how much noise they make, imagine the sound of a house alarm – and then double it. And double it again.)

There's an easy way to ward off these troublesome fairies. Keep a book of fairy tales beside your bed. There's enough magic on the pages of a single fairy tale to keep away a whole crowd of boggarts and bogles.

Magical fairy secrets

🌸 Think carefully before you leave out a present for a brownie. They love bread and milk, but if a human gives them anything else — such as chocolate, flowers or books — they get very cross.

🌸 If you're a dairy farmer, watch out for hobgoblins. They're very fond of making milk turn sour. (Hobgoblins can't resist tripping up old ladies either, so warn your grandma.)

🌸 Mermaids lure sailors towards them with a few twangs of a harp. If you hear beautiful music at sea, turn your boat round at once and sail the other way. Quick!

Chapter Five
Fairies and people

Ella pokes her tongue through the gap in her teeth and grins into the bathroom mirror. Then she peeps at the tiny treasure wrapped in tissue paper – her tooth. Ella giggles. She can hardly wait. Tonight, she'll go to bed without being asked. And tonight, she's determined to stay awake, to catch a glimpse of her favourite fairy. When the tooth fairy arrives, she'll be waiting.

Have you ever seen a fairy? If you have – congratulations! If you haven't yet – don't worry. They are very hard to find because they are so shy, and even harder to talk to. The best time to

see a fairy is when the fairy world touches the
human world ...

⭐ *Fairy friends*

The tooth fairy is one of the nicest fairies. She
spends her nights peeping under children's
pillows, checking to see if there's a tooth hidden
beneath. When she finds a tooth, the tooth
fairy is so delighted that she takes it, leaving
shiny coins in its place. The milk teeth that the
fairy collects are ground up and added to fairy
potions.

✫ Christmas fairies

Father Christmas has plenty of fairy friends to
help him – the elves! They
spend all year making presents for children, so it's no
wonder they don't have
time to visit. But next time
you open your Christmas
stocking, remember that
fairies helped to fill it.

✫ At the bottom of the garden

In 1917, Frances Griffiths and Elsie Wright took
the most amazing photos that the world had
ever seen. The pictures showed Frances and
Elsie playing with their fairy friends, who
danced, flew and played musical instruments.

Photography experts could find nothing
wrong with the photos – they had not been
tampered with in any way. Even Sir Arthur

Conan Doyle – who wrote the famous Sherlock Holmes detective novels – was totally convinced. But the human world was divided. Many people had never seen real fairies before and were amazed. Many more thought that the girls had played a trick. It was not until 1982, when Frances and Elsie were both old ladies, that they admitted the truth. The fairies were just paper cut-outs.

But fairy fans throughout the human world hope that one day they will see a real fairy, whether it's in a photo, on television or before their very eyes ...

⭐ So you want to be a fairy?

According to fairy legend, brownies are small, hard-working fairies. During the night, they flit through houses, dusting and cleaning here and scrubbing and polishing there.

Human Brownies have a lot in common with their fairy friends. They're always ready to help

– their motto is 'lend a hand'. And in some Brownie packs, each Brownie belongs to a group named after the fairy folk, including Elves, Fairies, Gnomes, Leprechauns, Pixies, Sprites and Imps.

Magical fairy secrets

✿ *Human brownies were not always called Brownies. When they were invented in 1914, they were known as Rosebuds.*

✿ *Humans, fairies, wizards and sprites appear in J. R. R. Tolkien's* The Lord of the Rings. *And, although dwarfs and elves are said to dislike each other, they become friends in this long – but very exciting – tale.*

✿ *Lots of girls' names have fairy meanings. Did you know that Ella means 'elf-like', Fay means 'fairy' or 'elf' and Tanya means 'fairy queen'?*

Chapter Six
Fairy-tale fairies

Cinderella sits in the cold, lonely kitchen, tears trickling down her cheeks. She so wants to go to the ball, to wear a beautiful dress, to dance with the prince ... but her mean stepsisters have stamped on her dreams. Again.

Suddenly, the kitchen fills with a soft, golden light. There, beside the unchopped vegetables stands the most kindly woman Cinderella has ever seen.

'Cheer up, Cinderella,' says the fairy godmother. *'You shall go to the ball.'*

A fairy tale is a tale of magic that has been told and retold for hundreds of years. And all the best fairy tales include a fairy – some are good and some are downright rotten. Which is your favourite fairy tale? Is it the story of Cinderella, whose fairy godmother helps her to meet her prince and live happily ever after? Or is it the story of the snoozing princess ...?

☆ The bad fairy and the good fairy

The story of Sleeping Beauty is a tale that is known throughout Fairyland. It tells of a baby princess who is cursed by a bad fairy – the princess will prick her finger and die on her sixteenth birthday. Luckily, a good fairy is there to cast another spell – that the princess will not die. She will fall into a deep sleep that will last one hundred years.

Everything happens as the fairies have
predicted until a prince wakes Sleeping Beauty
with a kiss. The princess is so delighted, she
marries him. Nearly everyone lives happily ever
after. All of the good fairies are invited to the
wedding. But the bad fairy is never seen again ...

⭐ A dream of a play

A Midsummer Night's Dream was written by William Shakespeare. The play has enchanted audiences for hundreds of years – and is so popular that it's still performed all over the world. Perhaps people cannot resist the magic that takes place when the human and fairy worlds meet . . .

One Midsummer's Night, while humans fall in and out of love and a group of bungling craftsmen rehearse a play, a battle is taking place in the fairy kingdom. Oberon and Titania – the fairy king and queen – are cross with each other. And because they are fairies, they argue with magic, not words. Oberon's mischievous servant – another fairy called Puck – rubs a special lotion on Titania's eyes. She will fall in love with the first person she lays eyes on. Unfortunately, this is a craftsman called Bottom who has, thanks to Puck, the head of an ass. Will all be well by morning . . .?

⭐ A flickering, flitting light

Tinker Bell is one of the most famous fairies of them all. She is a twinkly but tough fairy who doesn't stand for any nonsense. Tinker Bell first appeared in 1904, when she starred in J. M. Barrie's play of *Peter Pan* – the boy from Neverland who will not grow up.

Magical fairy secrets

❀ *Sleeping Beauty was transformed into a magical ballet in 1890. The music was written by Tchaikovsky and the dancing was choreographed by Marius Petipa. It is still performed today.*

❀ *German brothers Jacob Ludwig Carl Grimm and Wilhelm Carl Grimm collected some of the most well-known fairy tales ever, including* Cinderella, Beauty and the Beast *and* Snow White. *Jacob and Wilhelm became known as the Brothers Grimm.*

🌸 *Hans Christian Andersen was famous for his fairy tales. The Danish storyteller wrote* The Princess and the Pea, The Little Mermaid, Thumbelina *and many, many more.*

Chapter Seven
The essential fairy kit

The tiny fairy pulled back the rose petal that covered her and stood up from her bed of moss. It was time for work. She had lots to do today – enchanting grumpy people, rewarding kind people, scattering fairy dust … The list was endless. The fairy thought carefully. Should she wear lilac or green? Purple or blue? No, today she would wear her most favourite colour of all. Perfect, pretty pink!

Fairies adore clothes and they love accessories. In fact, they simply won't be seen without their essential fairy kit – a wand, a set of wings and a bag of magic dust.

☆ Fairy wings

For those fairies who have them, fairy wings come in all different shapes and sizes. Some are long and pointy, while others are curved like butterfly wings. They are all made from gossamer – a delicate, filmy material woven from the cobwebs of very small spiders.

When baby fairies appear, they already have a pair of tiny wings between their shoulders.

(Fairies are not born, like humans. They appear in a puff of magic.) These wings grow and grow until, by the time a fairy is about five years old, they have a fully grown set of fluttering wings. Best of all, they don't have to learn how to fly — they just can.

☆ Waving a magic wand

Number one on a fairy's list of must-have items is a wand. The fairy queen presents each fairy with a wand when they are old enough to control spells and enchantments — usually at the

age of about six. So what do they like to do with their wands? Well, not long ago, 3,000 fairies were asked to vote for their favourite spells. And here are the results:

1. Granting a wish.
2. Turning a sad face into a happy, smiling face.
3. Making a sunbeam.
4. Sending away rain clouds.
5. Turning a rosebud into a beautiful flower.

⭐ Fairy footsteps

Dwarfs and trolls wear boots that have been specially toughened with magic. They spend much of their time underground wading through squidgy mud, so it would be pointless wasting their gold on delicate shoes.

But winged fairies flit, float and fly — they rarely stomp or trudge. From time to time, they might land on a leafy tree or someone's shoulder — to whisper wishes into their ear. These fairies wear dainty shoes made of the finest fairy satin and tied with silk ribbons.

Top tip: Although fairy shoes do not come in sizes big enough for human feet, you could wear a pair of ballet slippers instead — they look just the same.

Magical fairy secrets

Fairy slippers are not something that a fairy wears on her feet. They're actually a type of orchid. Each plant grows just one magnificent pinky-purple flower.

❀ Acorn cups are the most popular type of fairy headgear. These are just the right size to fit tiny fairy heads and are as tough as cycle helmets. So, if a fairy accidentally flies into something, she'll be fine.

❀ One glittering particle of fairy dust is enough to make an entire class of children smile. Just imagine what fairies can do with a whole bag ...

Chapter Eight
A touch of fairy magic

Trees sway and leaves rustle. There's magic in the air. It rushes through the park and over the rooftops with a whoosh and a twinkle. Everything it touches suddenly seems to come alive. But what is behind the magic? Is it Mother Nature or Father Time? Is it a stray witch's cat on her way home? No... it's the fairies. They are busy casting spells and charms to make the world a more enchanting place.

Fairies are top of the class when it comes to casting spells. (Some say that they are even more magical than witches and wizards.) A fairy can bring a drooping plant back to life in a

twinkle. They can even send storm clouds away. Here are some magic secrets direct from Fairyland...

⭐ Magic leaves

Clover is an enchanted plant that grows in grassy places. Each tiny stem has three magical leaves, which fairies use to make everyday charms. However, when they are preparing extra-strong spells — such as changing frogs back into dashing princes — the fairies need something more powerful. They need the very rare and very precious four-leaf clover.

Four-leaf clovers nestle among patches of regular three-leaf clover. They're quite difficult to spot. But if you do find one, pick it, then press it between the covers of a heavy book. You'll be able to keep it forever. More importantly, the fairies will be able to sense its power from all around.

Fairy rings

You might have seen a mysterious fairy ring in a grassy meadow. From a distance, it looks like a large ring of dark green or brown grass, but up close you may see mushrooms around the edge too. Most fairy rings measure about two metres across, but some are much wider.

Fairy rings are very magical places. They are easy to step into – and very difficult to step out

of. But you can safely jump into and out of fairy rings as long as you remember these three rules:

1. Smile or laugh – happiness is stronger than the magic of the fairy ring.

2. Keep your fingers crossed – this will help to protect you against the enchantment.

3. If you are trapped inside the ring, spin round and say the magic words – *Turn about, turn about, let me out!* – and then jump as high as you can.

⭐ Stay away!

You might wish that a fairy would land on the pages of this book right now, so it may seem strange to include tips for keeping fairies away.

But just in case you are ever pestered by a pesky pixie (try saying that out loud!) or taunted by a troll, then here's how to send away troublesome fairies ...

Fairies do not like herbs, especially St John's wort and yarrow. If these are difficult to get hold of, then any herbs from the grocer's or supermarket will do. Hang a bunch of basil or mint above your bed before you go to sleep. You won't be bothered by unwanted guests ... and your room will smell delicious!

Magical fairy secrets

Fairies can be enchanted by other fairies to be trapped in a human home forever. The only way to help a trapped fairy is to give her a new set of clothes. She will be released from the spell and set free.

Fairies love glittery or shiny things. Look around the house and see if you can find something to catch the light — and a fairy's eye. Twinkly hair-bobbles and sparkly pendants are

perfect. When you wear them, fairies won't be able to resist coming closer to you.

If you ever want to encourage an Irish fairy to visit you, collect a bunch of shamrock leaves. They all love shamrock, especially leprechauns, who rarely leave home without one.

Chapter Nine
Looking for fairies

Seren sits patiently at the bottom of the garden and waits. Last year, when she had been eight years old, it had all been so easy. Fairies had leaped and played right under her nose. They'd threaded flowers into her hair and tickled her nose with feathers to make her laugh. This year is different. Where have all the fairies gone? Is she too old to see them? Then she sees the glint of a tiny wand out of the corner of her eye ...

Fairies are not as easy to see as a best friend or a furry pet. Sometimes, they are barely there. A twinkle of sunlight on a greenhouse or the fairy

lights on a Christmas tree may actually be evidence of a fairy's presence. And, as people get older, it becomes harder and harder to see fairies. Only true believers are able to hold on to the magic...

⭐ *Fairy spotting*

Even the most gifted of fairy fans may only glimpse a fairy once or twice in their lifetime. But many say that fairy spotting is a skill that

can be learnt. So, follow these extra-special instructions and you too might see a fairy:

1. Find a fairy zone somewhere at home. A fairy zone is an extra-special place where you feel comfortable and relaxed. (It is important to be calm for fairy spotting.) This could be a corner of your bedroom or the cupboard under the stairs. Try out a few places to see which feels the best.

2. Make sure you won't be disturbed by brothers and sisters, dogs, cats, parents with vacuum cleaners, etc.

3. In your fairy zone, sit with your legs crossed and your hands resting on your knees. Close your eyes and breathe deeply until you are totally relaxed.

4. Open your eyes and stare straight ahead – then wiggle your fingers. Focus on the very tips of your fingers. You'll need to learn how to watch at the very edges of your vision in order to see a fairy.

5. Remember that you may not see a sparkling fairy complete with wings and wand. Fairies are very shy – and very quick. You may only see a flash of light or hear a rustle of paper. But that's enough to show that a fairy has visited you.

⭐ Fairy time

Once you have practised your fairy-spotting technique in your own fairy zone, you're ready to look farther afield. And although fairies might visit you at any hour of the day or night, there is a really special time of day when they are most active – fairy time.

Fairy time is at dawn, when the sun is low in the sky and birds are just beginning to tweet. If you're ever awake at fairy time, then look carefully around your room, or peep out of your bedroom window. You never know what you might see …

Magical fairy secrets

🌸 A dandelion is the most magical flower ever. Wait until the petals drop off, then blow all the feathery seeds away with one big puff. And don't forget to make a wish!

🌸 Reading fairy tales is one of the best ways to prepare for fairy spotting. It helps to focus your mind.

🌸 Fairies feel very strongly about the world – it's their world too, after all – and they are terrific at recycling. Their clothes are often made of petals and leaves, and they drink out of buttercups. They get very cross if anyone drops litter in their woods or flower beds.

Chapter Ten
A magical fairy world

*I*f you love fairies, why not make your very own
fairy treasures? Then wherever you are, with just a
wave of a fairy wand and a sprinkle of fairy dust, you
can surround yourself with magic…

⭐ A magical fairy wand

If you want to try some fairy magic, you'll need
a fairy wand. And here's what you'll need to
make the essential fairy tool:

★ An old newspaper
★ Two pieces of A4 paper
★ A paintbrush
★ Pink and silver paint

* Sticky tape
* Glitter
* Glue
* A piece of tinsel
* A tiny twinkle of magic

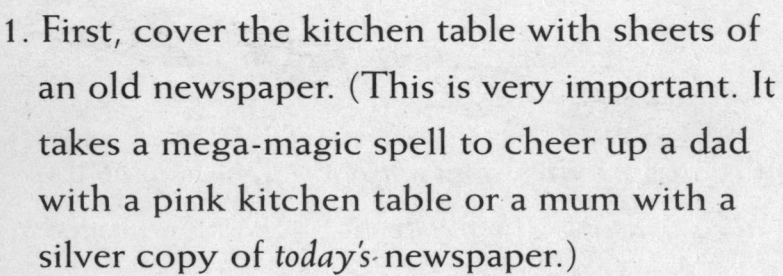

1. First, cover the kitchen table with sheets of an old newspaper. (This is very important. It takes a mega-magic spell to cheer up a dad with a pink kitchen table or a mum with a silver copy of *today's* newspaper.)
2. Cover one sheet of A4 paper with pink paint. Cover the other sheet with silver paint.
3. Wait for the paint to dry. (While this is happening, you could make up a fairy spell.)

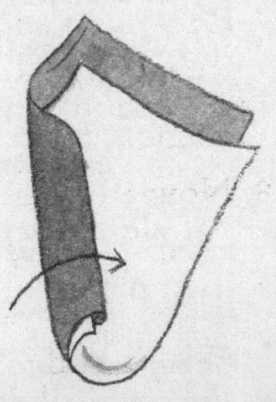

4. With white sides facing upwards, place one sheet on top of the other, with a 5 cm overlap.

5. Now tightly roll the two sheets together from one corner until you reach the other corner. Wrap a piece of sticky tape around the middle of the paper stick to make sure it doesn't unroll.

6. You should now have a beautiful pink-and-silver wand. Give it a quick wave. Can you feel a tingle in your fingertips?

7. Dab blobs of glue on your wand. (You must decide where to put them – it's all part of the magic.) Then sprinkle glitter on to the glue.

8. Now add a piece of twinkly tinsel or sparkly fur to the end of your wand. Wrap a piece of sticky tape around it to make sure that it doesn't budge.

Ta-daaaa! You are now the proud
owner of a magical fairy wand.
Remember to activate your
wand before trying to use it.
Whisper these enchanting
words three times...

With twinkles and spangles, I hereby bond
Magic and charm in this fairy wand.

⭐ *A magical bag of fairy dust*

Sometimes, a magic bag of fairy dust is all that
is needed to make someone smile. It could be a
friend – it might be you. Here's what you need:

* A circle of fabric, about 20 cm across
* A pencil
* A long piece of ribbon
* Scissors
* Glitter
* Tinsel
* Silver foil

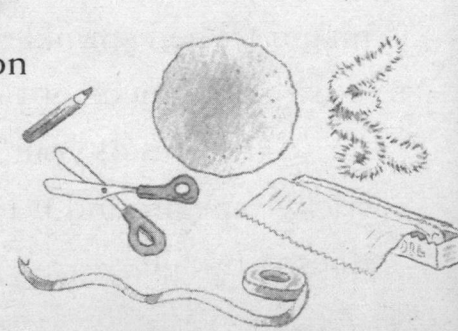

1. First, make the fairy bag that will hold your fairy dust. Spread the circle of fabric on a flat surface. (The fabric can be any sort, from a duster to a piece of sparkly material.) If the fabric has a pattern on one side, lay the pattern face down on the surface.

2. Draw an even number of pencil marks around the circle. These should be about 3 cm from the edge of the fabric.

3. Ask an adult to cut a 1 cm slit wherever there is a pencil mark.

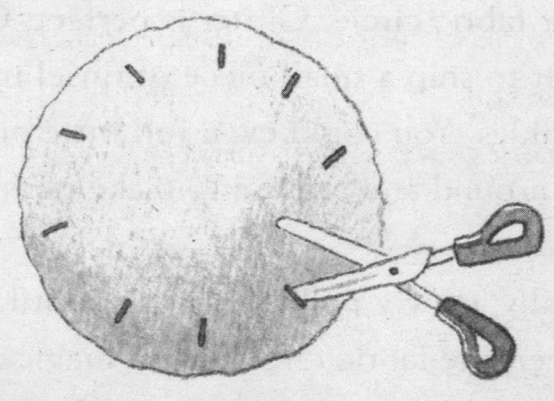

4. Turn the circle over, so that the pattern (if there is one) faces up.

5. Carefully thread the ribbon into one hole and out of the next, continuing right round the circle.

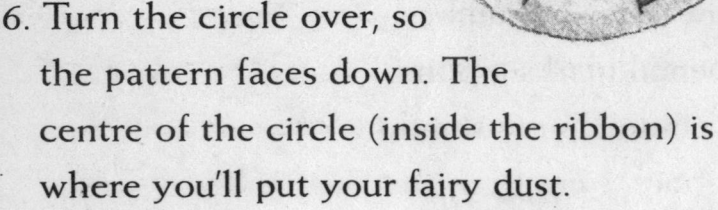

6. Turn the circle over, so the pattern faces down. The centre of the circle (inside the ribbon) is where you'll put your fairy dust.

7. Making fairy dust is fantastic fun! All you have to do is sprinkle the most glittery and shiny things you can find into the middle of your fabric circle. Glitter is perfect. Or ask an adult to snip a small piece of tinsel into teeny twinkles. You could even roll little pieces of foil around and around to make perfect pixie baubles.

8. Finally, slowly pull the ribbons until you've turned the fabric circle into a magical fairy

bag. Then tie the bag shut and keep your
fairy dust safe and sound.

When you want to make a
wish, close your eyes and
shake your fairy-dust bag. If
you wish hard enough,
even the tiniest sprinkles
of fairy magic should be
enough to make your wish come true.

⭐ *A fantastic fairy bookmark*

This fairy bookmark is perfect for keeping your
place in this book – or your favourite fairy tale.
You will need:

* ★ Silver foil
* ★ A piece of car
* ★ Cl

1. Carefully crumple a piece of silver foil. (This must be big enough to wrap around the piece of card.)

2. Gently smooth out the foil. It will be quite wrinkled, but this is just what you need.

3. Dab glue all over the piece of card – on both sides.

4. Place the card on to the dull side of the foil. Then wrap the foil around the card, making sure that the foil sticks.

5. Now, trace the beautiful fairy outlines on to tracing paper with a pencil. Or, if you have magic in your fingers, copy the picture straight on to a piece of paper.

6. Colour in the fai⋯⋯h felt-tip ⋯⋯ the